# Eclipse

## Darkness in Daytime

by Franklyn M. Branley    illustrated by Donald C

**Thomas Y. Crowell    New York**

# Other Recent Let's-Read-and-Find-Out Science Books® You Will Enjoy

The Beginning of the Earth • The Sun: Our Nearest Star • Dinosaur Bones • Glaciers • Snakes Are Hunters • Danger—Icebergs! • Comets • Evolution • Rockets and Satellites • The Planets in Our Solar System • The Moon Seems to Change • Ant Cities • Get Ready for Robots! • Gravity Is a Mystery • Snow Is Falling • Journey into a Black Hole • What Makes Day and Night • Air Is All Around You • Turtle Talk • What the Moon Is Like • Hurricane Watch • Sunshine Makes the Seasons • My Visit to the Dinosaurs • The BASIC Book • Bits and Bytes • Germs Make Me Sick! • Flash, Crash, Rumble, and Roll • Volcanoes • Dinosaurs Are Different • What Happens to a Hamburger • Meet the Computer • How to Talk to Your Computer • Rock Collecting • Is There Life in Outer Space? • All Kinds of Feet • Flying Giants of Long Ago

The *Let's-Read-and-Find-Out Science Book* series was originated by Dr. Franklyn M. Branley, Astronomer Emeritus and former Chairman of the American Museum-Hayden Planetarium, and was formerly co-edited by him and Dr. Roma Gans, Professor Emeritus of Childhood Education, Teachers College, Columbia University. For a complete catalog of Let's-Read-and-Find-Out Science Books, write to Thomas Y. Crowell Junior Books, Harper & Row, Publishers, Inc., 10 East 53rd Street, New York, NY 10022.

1  2  3  4  5  6  7  8  9  10
Revised Edition

Library of Congress Cataloging-in-Publication Data
Branley, Franklyn Mansfield, 1915–
   Eclipse: darkness in daytime.

   (A Let's-read-and-find-out science book)
   Summary: Explains in simple terms what happens during a solar eclipse.
   I. Eclipses, Solar—Juvenile literature.  [1. Eclipses, Solar]  I. Crews, Donald, ill.  II. Title.  III. Series.
   QB541.5.B73  1988        523.7'8        87-47692
   ISBN 0-690-04617-0
   ISBN 0-690-04619-7 (lib. bdg.)

   "A Harper Trophy book"
   "A Let's-read-and-find-out book"
   ISBN 0-06-445081-3 (pbk.)        87-45276

# Eclipse
## Darkness in Daytime

Sometimes the moon hides the sun.

The sky gets dark, almost as dark as night. But it is still daytime.

There is a total solar eclipse. Solar means "of the sun," and eclipse means "to overshadow or leave out."

There is darkness in daytime.

A glow of bright light is around the moon. It is called the solar corona, or the "sun's crown."

During the eclipse, the brightest stars come out.
Squirrels and woodchucks get ready to sleep. Birds
and chickens go to roost, just as they do at night.
If it is springtime, tree frogs start peeping.

Animals are surprised when darkness comes in daytime. Long ago, people were also surprised. Eclipses frightened them.

People thought a dragon in the sky was taking away the
sun, eating it bite by bite. The sun might be gone forever.

Everyone made a lot of noise. They shouted and yelled, blew horns and stamped the ground. If they could frighten the dragon, it would spit up the sun.

That's what the dragon did every time. The sun returned.
So people continued to believe in the legend of the eclipse
dragon.

Eclipses are not always total. When the moon hides only
part of the sun, there is a partial eclipse. The sky does not
get very dark.

Because the sky is still light, we cannot see the rest of the
moon—only the part that covers the sun.

Sometimes a ring of the sun can be seen around the moon. Then there is an annular eclipse. Annular means "ring shaped."

The sun is about 400 times bigger than the moon. So how can the moon cover it?

You can find out.

Hold a penny between your thumb and first finger. Move the penny in front of your eye while you look at a car across the street.

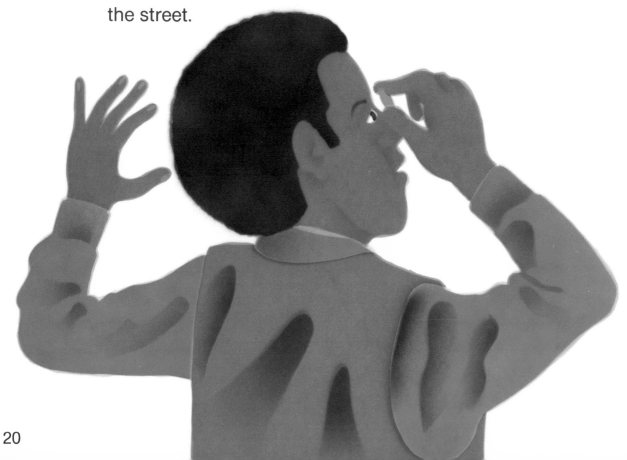

When the penny is close to your eye, it covers the whole car. Yet the penny is much smaller than the car. It seems to cover the car because the penny is much closer to your eye.

That's the way it is with the sun and the moon.

The moon is much closer to us than the sun—about 400 times closer. The moon is so close to us, it seems to be the same size as the sun. During a total solar eclipse it hides the sun.

The moon always makes a shadow. At least twice every year, and sometimes as often as five times a year, the shadow falls toward Earth. When it does there is an eclipse.

As the moon moves, so does the shadow. The dark part of the shadow makes a narrow path across the Earth. It is the eclipse path. People in the path see a total eclipse. People in the lighter part of the shadow see a partial eclipse.

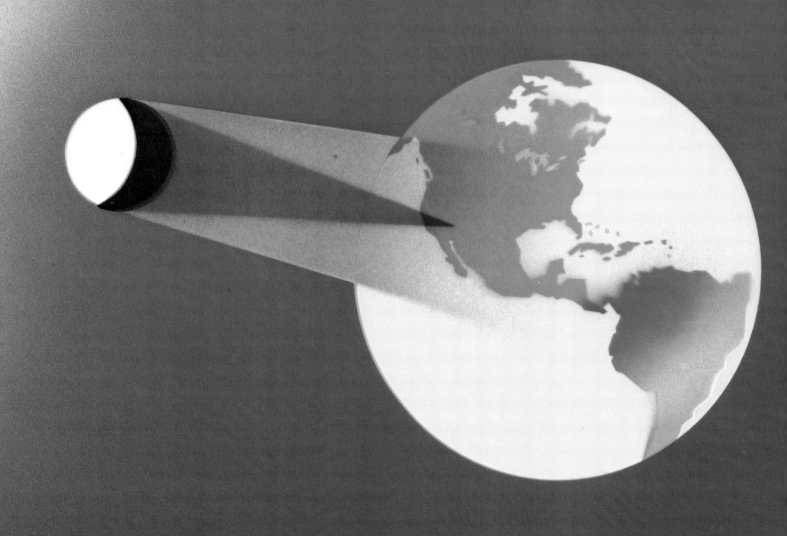

Astronomers know when there will be an eclipse and where the shadow will fall. They can figure out the exact hour of an eclipse, even one that will happen hundreds of years from now. They also know when eclipses happened long ago.

There was one in North America in 1204 B.C., more than 3000 years ago. We wonder who was here to see it. Since then there have been thousands of eclipses. This is the path of an eclipse that crossed Canada in 1972.

On April 8, 2024, an eclipse shadow will travel this path across the United States. How old will you be when you see this eclipse?

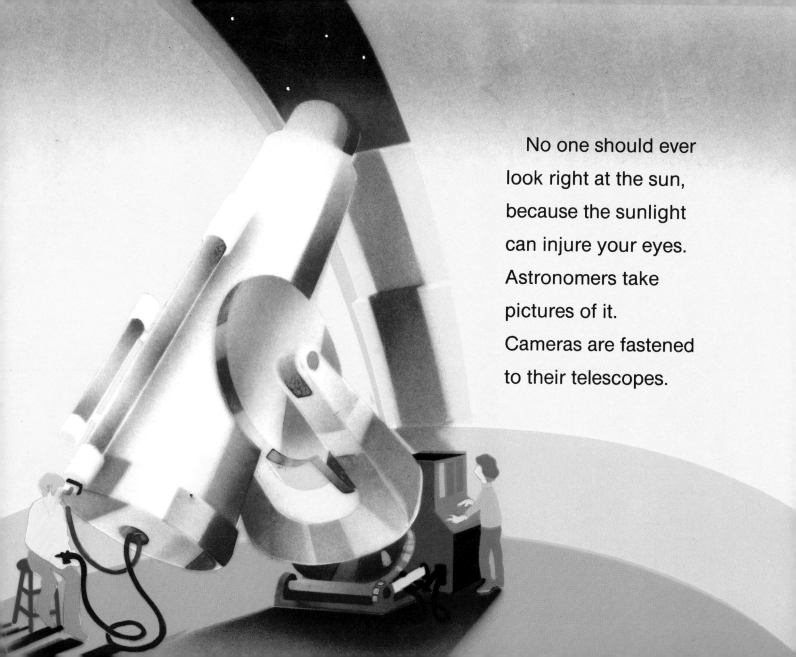

No one should ever look right at the sun, because the sunlight can injure your eyes. Astronomers take pictures of it. Cameras are fastened to their telescopes.

You can see a picture of the sun by making a sun projector. Push a pin through the center of a piece of cardboard about twice the size of this book. Turn the pin so the hole has no rough edges.

With your back to the sun, hold the projector at your shoulder so sunlight shines through the hole. Hold another piece of cardboard in your other hand. This is the screen. Adjust both cards until you see a small image of the sun on the screen.

Use the sun projector when there is an eclipse. You can see the whole eclipse on the screen. And there will be no danger to your eyes.

Astronomers take their telescopes and cameras all over the world to get into the eclipse path. Then, if there are no clouds, they can take pictures.

Total eclipses don't last very long. After two or three minutes they are over. A five-minute total eclipse would be a long one.

To see an eclipse you have to be in the right place at the right time. And the sky must be clear.

If you are in Colombia, South America, on February 26, 1998, you will see a total solar eclipse.

You'll also be able to see one in the southern United States on August 21, 2017. On April 8, 2024, there will be an eclipse from Texas to Maine. The shadow will go right through New York City.

Millions of people will see darkness in daytime. Maybe you will too.

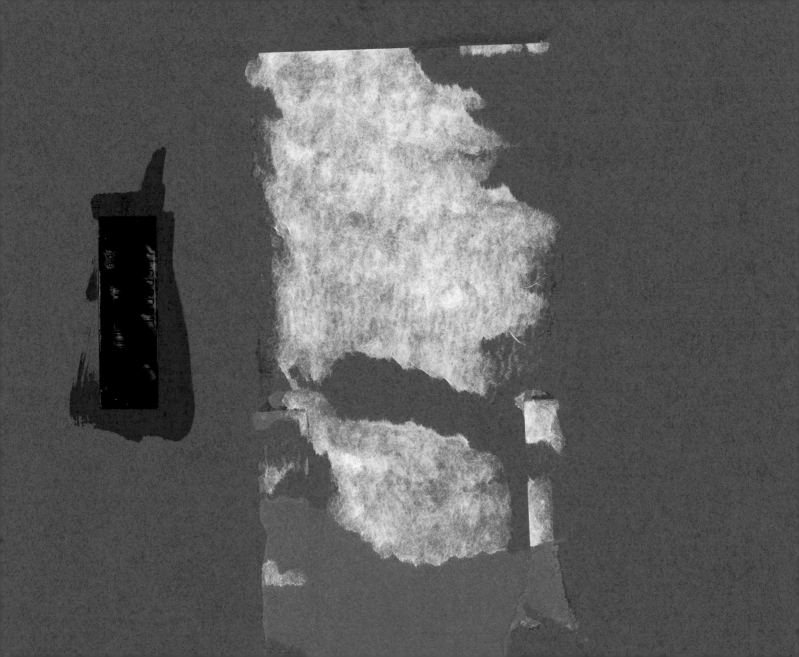